GW01180059

# The Cult of What Comes Next

Also by S. K. Kelen

*Atomic Ballet*
*Dingo Sky*
*Trans-Sumatran Highway and other Poems*
*Dragon Rising*
*Shimmerings*
*Goddess of Mercy*
*Earthly Delights*
*Island Earth: New & Selected Poems*
*Yonder Blue Wild*
*Love's Philosophy: a Selection of Sonnet-like Creatures*
*A Happening in Hades*

# The Cult of What Comes Next

S. K. Kelen

Puncher & Wattmann

© 2025 S. K. Kelen

This book is copyright. Apart from any fair dealing for the purposes of study and research, criticism, review or as otherwise permitted under the Copyright Act, no part may be reproduced by any process without written permission. Inquiries should be made to the publisher.

First published in 2025
Published by Puncher & Wattmann
PO Box 279
Waratah NSW 2298

info@puncherandwattmann.com

NATIONAL
LIBRARY
OF AUSTRALIA

A catalogue record for this book is available from The National Library of Australia.

ISBN 9781923099579

Cover design by David Musgrave, cover photograph by the author.

Printed by Lightning Source International

# Contents

## Saga



## The Cult of What Comes Next

Saga

# Falling Down

Recall a distant past life a victorious lion
Killing his vanquished rival's cubs and you are
Part of the dwindling litter, time's run out;
Dumb incomprehension prefigures the swift claws,
Bloody fangs, a roaring dance with the undone,
Suddenly the reverie at the red meat party
Fades and a Spartan kitten claws your guts
From the inside out; the way the world ends
Soon forgotten when you are bits and pieces
Trying not to fall apart, falling down the blue day
A cartoon character grabbing a ladder made of air–
Far below the future waits disguised as scenery
Meet the sweetest boulder the valley
Has to offer visitors: a home away.

# Empirical Insomniac

Restless, trying to remember the mislaid
Word that means unable to sleep,
Awake all night flexing a tired brain;
Trying to remember makes things worse
– a simple word on the tip of your tongue.
Only a few syllables. 4 am
Stirred from dozing off anxious to recall.
Observe if more words slip away,
Will learn from experience and this is called—
Another word lost in the fog, a studied word.
How many novels read or movies watched,
Their titles forgotten, plots and characters waylaid?
To revive you need read and watch them all again.
Aware this experiment is running on empty
A working theory, a process redolent of empires.

# Swords and Sorcery

A golden age, until blood explodes from jugulars.
The softcore barbaric boudoir scene brings respite;
Brutal magic augurs bright costumes and
(somewhat) redeems a dark plot, then a fast pike
Pierces the heart erupts red geyser.
Eureka the talking bird is happy with the lawlessness.
Today, rifles march to the capital
The future's wings beat nearer and look up
Amazed how high the sky is—o wondering dilletante
Gild the frilly lily, such princely pretension
No longer be mad, bad and dangerous, know
The dream home is a creaking hillside house
Where wolves are hiding, foxes cry, they're all
Lost now: out of town the highway road kill.

# Arrival

Home and all in one peace (sic)
vacation accomplished (tick)
sights seen, map and itinerary fulfilled
how the august traveller learns humility;
the journey's end was elegant.

Home where computers and appliances
are our friends—be words advertising
be bright light, ah, television's
dead stare, all night canned laughter
bounces off a gondolier's oar
sings like Caruso
vanished behind a theatre,
Pagliacci's exorcism he will
haunt your dreams, Scooby Doo.

# Missive

Dear ______, thank you, life is spinning out of control
the cat tore the voodoo doll you sent to pieces —
no fear of toys or superstition here!
and then vicious emails arrived like stalkers
started to get nasty. The private detective
you had follow me came in handy and
took care of (punched out) the roaring psycho
who harangued the shoppers and school kids
at the shopping centre after he screamed at me
about my dog sitting at my feet outside the cafe.
The afternoon descended into action comedy
but at sunset the red Belconnen sky
was numinous and, full of hope,
embraced the busy surface of the earth.

## Under Water (1985: en route to the Philippines)

Off-duty crew bunked down, glad to be silent underwater
safe from Soviet sensors. Someone stowed a cat aboard
the entire boat stinks of cat. Captain doesn't overly care
what with half the crew angel-dusted and the air conditioning
spitting traces of powder. The sonarmen laugh themselves
in stitches at the sonar's silly bleeps. Captain enters thoughts
in his journal, *In the homeland we defend it is Friday*
*0600 hours the country's favourite weekday, here the crew*
*look forward to sport via satellite and love on video*
*until we make port where the locals will feel discipline*
*unleashed full drunk and shouting, lust and brutality win*
*our fleet the required respect.* Farther out and further deep
mermaids still sing of Davey Jones' brutish locker.
Bleep bleep

# Travel Back to 1996

Back to a day in 1996, when lightning struck the plane
The actors were aboard, flying Canberra to Chicago
Before the stopovers at Sydney then LA.
In Chicago the ice sculptures in front of the grey hotels melted.
It was only the beginning of January when the freeze
Should be deepening. It was a sign.
The Mid-West was still properly cold,
Though this cold was relict of the majestic freeze
Years before when you could rely on old Jack Blizzard
To ice the land to thirty-five below,
Shift walls of ice and snow
Help the glaciers expand and the chill flow
From Montana, snap freeze the Missouri.
Not much ice these days, won't be till after people go.

# lines from an older draft

Still, a glacier or two
Shifted a wall of ice and snow to help the chill flow
Through Montana, to the Dakotas and Minnesota.
Not now, of course, but then Jack Blizzard was alive and rampant
Winter froze the mid-west; snow days were a majesty.
The Missouri River was a grinding, gangling god of ice,
Today a frozen Coke must suffice.

# 1996

*1996: watching the news on a TV at the airport*
*(worse than the dark days of Febuary and libary)*
Even air changed, felt soggy, people spoke a new tongue,
dropping r from words. On TV the newly-minted
opposition leader said he was 'bought up' with values
and the newsreader crossed to a live 'boadcast' of Pine
Minister 'beefed' by his department. The airport food
tasted like tyre burnouts and everyone mumbled
as if the letter r never existed, people were friendly
but their eyes were harder than they had been
things were bright-coloured, shiny with swagger
the daytime sky was darker blue you sat still, the
universe was shifting, speech abbeviated. Today,
smiley emoji augur a new world, its decline began
when 'r' vanished from the tongue.

# Earth One

Wandering in a happy state
'twixt trance and stupor
a warm day's good humour

hiking in the bush makes one intimate
with the Earth, deeply bucolic: fresh air,
incessant bush. Melt into the landscape,

then grow from an Australian seed,
sand and quartz stones concentric circles
the ground is endless mandala or a bullseye—

insect and snake tracks, branches, leaves,
dewy spider webs and stripe-legged spiders
pawprints, wombats' debris,

wallaby and kangaroo pellets—
at the centre is old man banksia
standing motionless.

Bull ants ran up your arms you were animal again,
no lizard, snake, bird or marsupial to be seen
sense their eyes watching.

Tripped on a rock near Devil's Staircase
can't stop running down an old fire trail,
momentum down the mountain

saw over sheer cliffs down
to the valley arrived to
whipbirds whistling song.

# Melatonin, Valerian Forte

Suddenly remembered the word, insomniac,
And just about to sleep then forgot the names
Of things that used to help sleep: fancy
Words from a pharmacy or a revenge tragedy
Perhaps they had not gone too far away.
Once one word blunders off more follow
Irrevocably, it seems. That's how it feels
When the names of friends you haven't seen
For a while or so, verge on the tip of your tongue
In a distant recess along with a memory of someone
That should be there vanished beyond reach or care,
Till now; *should know* doesn't cut it and hope
They've forgotten your name too and share a
Laugh at Time's remorseless teasing.

# Quiet Times

## The Corridor

Flocks of birds cavort over a playing field scores of cockatoos fly kamikaze style the kookaburra's laugh made everyone laugh. In those days you always saw kookaburras near the oval. Imagined panthers, bears' shadows from jungly stories, secret maps, telescopes and curiosity. Truly happy, when the clouds clear the long ago seems so near only happy times remain until the world flickers on again, it's old now, the furniture comes into focus—and memories, ah— grapevines' shadows twist across the ceilings. Recognise loved ones' voices, their children running down the corridor.

## The Problem With Today's Youth

Some children do not know spring cleaning advances the spirit and helps them grow.Those messy lives reflect their desks and rooms. The lucky ones' practical epiphanies told them grow up and tidy up. Others turned to the pure chaos of street life, and extremes—for those who have not cleaned up their act it's never too late let your mama crack the whip. It's similar for cats tiger balm rubbed in fur keeps fleas hopping, and so on. Homespun wisdom every damned thing.

## Earthlings

the world's idiot arithmetic balance sheets kill the Earth fire and
ice (melting) the day icebergs bring snow to the tropics, fireworks
= a golden fountain (atmosphere burns) end of the world will be
a beautiful, sunny day, at the end you might recall 'we had a lot of
luck on Venus' or remember nothing much at all. Run to the hills,
really sitting in front of the television change channel return home

the fecund garden sweet, a kind of heaven wild blossoming & bees. Watch the Earth from space beautiful cloud swirl, farewell squabbling earthlings. The human mission kill all life on earth no one nothing to stop them. Not unhappy to say goodbye to all this it's her children and grandchildren that she'll miss. Sad, the

# Ruins

Two young bronzewing pigeons bob up and down
on the neighbour's roof, peck at food that isn't there
their tails fan open as their heads straighten up.
Is this a crested pigeon team meeting
or just the young birds practising eating?
A feeding fox-trot? Courtship ritual?
The bird watcher still cared about his cat
was sad for the humans; so many had sickened
and died after the climatic climacteric, a cruel
confluence of disease and disaster Mother Nature
provided and the survivors seemed resigned
to whatever fate awaited them. They were quiet
and humble in the world, unlike before
when they owned all and their machines roared.

# Chornobyl's Special Babies

Next we meet Chornobyl's special babies:
a centaur-boy whose hind legs didn't work,
a little girl whose brain was a separate chamber
growing from the back of her head, the kids born
with third-degree burns that no poultice
could cool just cry or stare. 'These things
happen anyway, anywhere, but not so many,
not all the time.' The doctor who cares for the children
is a saint, she tucks their brief lives in bed at night
and she expects to die like Madame Curie.
Background radiation, and isotopes in the sick soil
and water table stay to punish generations.
Embalmed in lead and concrete, the two surviving
reactor cores hold 97% of the original fuel load.

# Machine Code

Friendly apes are gone so our closest living relatives are cars and
office equipment, mobile phones and machinery
resemble in almost every way the sweet innocents:
televisions and washing machines from the 1960s. We are all the same.
Diffracted atmosphere plus dangerous ego: the graphics interface
we write the application to be object animal or,
moonlit with power, patterns can inhabit the persons,
make sure that happens
now complicate so return where gravity left off
people to contain what's left breathe the polyhedrons, are
silence link by vapour the pixels
night enthralled, Dear ... seamlessly will
you light up the forms, assign them characters
let polyhedrons make each idea,
dots and lines, up or down, left or right
And fill the sky o algorithm
Do it now, happy creators of many darknesses
go world grow on the screen be like a tree
and released from gravity, the atmosphere floats free
wait forever, forever has arrived.

# Arch Monsters

There are episodes you're glad you missed
like the drowned zombies who reside in caves
hidden in the rocky cliffs along the coast.
People see bubbles in the water then they emerge
come ashore at odd unpredictable places.
Sometimes they take a child from a playground,
a backyard or swimming place, or haunt
shopping centres late afternoon
when a straggler's friends have headed home
one bite and a young life of play is gone.
These monsters range far inland similar to saltwater crocs,
some have connections high-up and live in dreams.
Because demons are not mentioned in any statute
authorities leave them alone they tell anxious parents
they'll investigate but they don't or won't.
What happened that day on the way home from school:
a lifetime of night terrors and blank memories await
the lucky ones who escaped a monsters' embrace.
What makes a creature wish to hurt and humiliate?

# Another Dynamo Song

Thinking can clutter, do more harm than good.
The print of a painting of uniformed dogs
sitting up, drinking and smoking, playing cards
in the stationmaster's office at the railway station–
you are unbalanced whenever that picture comes to life.
Telegraph poles form hieroglyphs, buildings dance
and near the sea baby footprints appear in the sand
running inland, free the mind of every thought,
hear time's wingèd chariot rushing nearby
obeying only the quest's demands, a quest
to understand things; each time someone
dives in the surf, a dynamo sings.

# The Twenty-One

The old Police rapid response 'Flying Squad',
A unit with a hard reputation was disbanded
By the 1980s (too many officers turned to the dark side).
They were a tough bunch, a law unto themselves
And their unconventional style of policing
Could be violent, at times criminal, a danger to the public.
Now they exist as fading spectral memory and
They just pulled into your driveway parking old model
Unmarked light blue Holden and Falcon prowl cars
Identifiable by brutal upholstery and a March 1975
Rego sticker in the lower left corner of the windscreen.
On vacation from Hell, they are here to bust your
Sorry arse for your bo-wo-whiney bitch act of a life,
The detectives' eyes light up like flaming tyres

# Junior School End Of Year Concert and Prize Giving

Standing as still as possible in a straggly line
the prize winners waited for their names to be called.
The Principal handed out certificates to the children:
for brilliant reading, for helping in class, for paying attention,
for speaking good words, for being quiet when someone else is talking,
for always being polite, House points for the best listening,
for tidying up, for trying hard at maths, for being good in class,
for beautiful painting, for singing in tune, for standing still in line,
for most improved at English, for good handwriting, for running fast;
and to a little boy who had recently moved with his family from China.
It was the end of the year and he'd just turned five
the youngest in kindergarten and he could not see with his eyes.
The Principal called his name to come up to the stage
to get his certificate for good story telling.
A teacher and some of his friends offered to guide him
he smiled and we parents heard him quietly say,
thank you but I know the way. All the girls from years K to 2
shooshed us then tried not to cry because they loved him
and every boy from years K to 2 nodded with respect,
looked around fiercely to make sure everyone behaved,
they watched out for him; the boy who needed no one's help
walked up the steps and beaming like a lion received his prize,
stood proudly with his classmates.

# Red Eye Teddy Boys

Red-eyed teddy-boys tarting in clubland
lived in the cave their lives had become;
drank the storm till there was a cyclone
blowing through the mind; too far gone
from meaningful so go home
get your act together, cook and tend the yard
mind the children; the car garaged
and safe from them; don't eat or drink too much;
locked down notice; the Earth heats up
time goes faster; in the world of events
how more and more things make less sense;
'greed is good', 'war is peace' must be true
Peace facilitates clear intelligence,
shifts the ordering of smokescreen physics.

# Viral Intelligence

Say nothing and the power of the wind feeds
darkness, dangerous thoughts enthral,
return to a place buried deep where different lives
wait to be released and they can inhabit a breath,
breathe what's left of the atmosphere,
aware there are others in the world
tripping light fantastic can happily dissolve.
Cool vapour rises and diffracted light
reveals clustering polyhedrons and each is a
person, animal, tree, an idea, or big things
like gravity, and life itself, trillions of polyhedrons
join together to seamlessly upgrade reality,
we ask only that you make a lifelike world
resemble the one we knew, where we liked living.

# Afterlife

*Here you are, you are here – X marks the spot –*
the guardian pointed at the map.
*Your soul is reduced from its inner glow to a sub-nanometre energy particle*
*maintaining cognitive integrity. Indeed, capacity lost*
*due to aging, injury, sickness and death is restored, virtually.*
And yes, you felt like your old sprightly self.
She continued: *the inhabitants of a necropolis are transported*
*as nano-dots and entered on a sheet of vellum:*
*infinitesimal points put together*
*make letters and punctuation add up to words*
*and sentences, and sometimes musical notation*
*(life is a flawed metaphor for pure truth, afterlife*
*works like a simile for life). Thus billions of souls*
*exist in a volume of existences who have exited the world*
*with farewells and see you later.*
*You end up in a book,* she said, *a living book,*
*but a tome for the dead. Here you get to live again.*
*Within its pages is space as large and old as the universe*
*where you might hope to find a home in the clouds,*
*perhaps your Lord's mansion or reclining with your heart's desire,*
*a tranquil place by a river or the sea*
*or the scene of great victory*
*time to reflect, rejoice and regret.*
*Some souls end up in a starlit ballroom, dancing through eternity*
*others are released and recycled into new existences*
*get another chance in life and eventually earn a pass into Nirvana.*
*Every soul finds its own destination in the chapter where it's meant to be*
*Heaven or Hell or Oblivion or Other: in your heart*
*you always knew where you were headed.*

*Seeing the light, it is Judgement Day or Angel Night or a seat on an early flight*
*to reality.* Humbly, you submitted, if given the opportunity, you could
make a better go of things, do some good with another life,
and the soul yearned to greet the morning sun.

# Love Lockdown

Over the phone an uncalled for speech:
*You spend too much time at home*
*with your better half, such a waste.*
*Get out of the house post-haste,*
*attend your lover or lose her!*
Over the back fence, run the gauntlet
sirens wailing, ha ha, chased down
by the Love Police.

# The Cult of What Comes Next

# Guignol

Driving in search of the address we'd been given
it was a night of wrong turns and misdirection
but you had to laugh– one way streets going
the wrong way– the street directory
gave no clue– roads blocked for repairs and maintenance–
so we kept driving to the end of City Road
before it turned into highway
where we'd turn around
head back and start again but a shadow came into view
dancing circles round a concrete power pole
we got closer and saw a man trying
to run away from the power pole.
Stopped the car, wound down the window
heard two distinct voices whispering loudly through his lips.
One voice said, *I don't want to be here,*
the second voice hissed, *yes you do.*
He runs back, magnetised by a concrete power pole,
runs in concentric circles, clockwise then anticlockwise
the pole pulls him back with a powerful gravity,
and bumps hard. Tries to sneak away
without the pole noticing but the pole whispers, *Come hither, come to me,*
and he runs and slams his head. Ow! it hurts like a brick wall
punching him in the face. What it's like when an object
takes your fancy and you must have it.
A door appeared in his molten view– here one moment gone the next,
and here again– no wall or roof just the door and frame,
from the other side deep nothing radiated bitter cold,
the door slammed open and shut,
accompanied by brutal giggling from forgotten nightmares, circus music
played on an out of tune pianola a garage full of clowns egged him on,
shivering and his teeth grinding in the deep-freezing swirl,
if only he could bolt the door, just slam it,

the swirl would stop, he tries to get away– *run, run, run,*
the electricity in the powerlines sparks and addles the brain,
feet carry him back to the dance with the power pole.
This was ages ago, a full-moon night, we were students
driving to a party when we saw this bloke flinging himself at a power pole.
We stopped. 'Get in the car,' one of the girls said, 'we'll drop you home or
wherever you like,' he got in the back seat, ectoplasm
sweating from his pores, his eyes popped like periscopes.
'Thanks,' he said, we drove two minutes till he stammered, 'You better stop
and take me back.' 'Are you sure?' He nodded frantically.
We drove back, dropped him off. 'I'll be fine,' he said
but didn't look fine at all;
he sprinted to the pole resumed his dance. Head bang crash.
Hopefully it'll be out of his system by morning. We'd seen worse,
and would forget about him soon enough,
not as quickly as he'd forget us.
Years in the future I recalled that strange night, could hear from way back then
a loud whisper, *Come hither,* a molten door materialised and I fell in
tumbled an eternity, landed on the footpath, began to dance
in circles, my head smacked into the power pole–
*bwang*– so stuck in the wild past, circling a power pole and the spectre
laughing, drove off with my girlfriends, his left hand
held the steering wheel, right hand waved a one-finger
salute; a crazed being wishing only to party.

# A Door Appears

A door materialises, you arrive from the future,
old and unafraid, think what the hell,
time to take a plunge and walk right in.
For a few moments the life flashing before one's eyes
actually happens, it seems to take the best part of eternity
a long cool inhalation of the quiet life idealised
at times realised, regret sets in: ah too many tempests
and what goes wrong and comes between.
Remembered people and places bring a sweet torment—
any pain caused others is calculated
an infernal sum involving exponentials, plus
Fibonacci Numbers grown over years gone by
so it ends up hurting you as much as you hurt them,
the bill is sent and you must pay it
whatever ways the powers that be see fit
before memory is wiped and it's time
to climb back up the rabbit hole.

# The Lords of Gleam

thank the lords of gleam
and electrons for technology
we hold before us, one day soon
technology is all we will be

# Fundamentals

Promising an invisible world and the inspiration
for so much great art and passionate music,
believing at its best is, as the bearded red god said,
the kind heart of a cold world, comforting opiate
and a warm spin on oblivion, the wishful way
to make sense of goodbye. But those millions
slaughtered in Truths' many names make Heaven
hard to fathom. Is Paradise hell for enemies?
The world is flat, the centre of the universe
where wise men say if you kill for a sanctified cause
all your sins and misdemeanours are forgiven.
Ignorance with *attitude* keeps us all fighting wars.
Still, I pray for Peace and Rain, sleep with angels,
thank Heaven every time disaster's averted.

# Boot Splash

Boot splash

Water ripple

four fishes' eyes

            bulge    stare up

bent water         circles   boot splash

sand rocks scrub

                        hard-needled shrub

blister red flowers          spike the track

                                                tough casuarina

is gentle she-oak                                    distant

                        the tall tree sky  the honey tasting air melts

                                    into water    down river   from the dam

            A mountain smiles & up above

                                    thunder laughs            ka-boom.

# Haiku Fever

## The Deep Past

ate flying saucers
a final taxi upward
spiral flight nowhere

## Dieback

doom car doom music
flocks love to fly oh bright birds
trees dieback is now

## Invasion of the Brushtail Possums (Part 2)

hard rain crazed possum
invades through open window
it wants to live here

## Domestic Pets

training cat to be
watchdog a well rounded cat
dog to train as cat

## Like a French Poet

suburban Rimbaud
departed the scene to coach
his kids' football team

## Forgetting to take memory Pills

they can't remember
if they took the memory pills
that makes things hard to

## Pokémon

Pokémon sneak in
happy home demon swap cards
obsess the children

## Brainwashed

can think of nothing
else strange numbers fill glazed eyes
obscure energies

## Braindead

beyond redemption
o reptile mind and heart beat
laudanum bliss night

## Flying Squad Haiku Number One

flying squad ends up
in Hades blinking cats' eyes
see things at angles

## Spike

our kids are messy
yet Spike the ancient bulldog
keeps his kennel clean

## In the Midnight Chakra

burning the midnight
chakras outside in the news
assassins run wild

## The Lovers Plan To Meet in Heaven

one day there will be
an atom that is you plus
atom that is me

## Great Lesson

the secret of good
health is only take poison
once a week strictly

## The Wisdom of the Orient

toy orangutans
and toy tigers teach us to
love the rainforest

## Why People Prefer Streaming TV to So Much Modern Poetwee

too much *me me me*
and not enough negative
capability

## At the Copacabana

you blazing bird-shark
learn jungle theory turn on
your inner strobe light

## Note on Fridge

go out and have fun
I'll get the housework done signed
blue tongue lizard mum

## Asthma Relief Patrol

rain settles pollen
walk and breathe deeply
life is beautiful again

## Space Guard

no air force can stop
a comet kissing Earth first
law of splatmatics

## The Prince of Desperation

waits till family
are dead and gone then murders
them in his memoirs

## Divine Wind

young kamikaze
reincarnates as a moth
who loves candle flames

## Only the Lonely

this loneliness is
ivy caged a sad grey bird
flies into winter

## Patong City

two clever beggars
on the strip ferocious smiles
karma in Phuket

# Trapped Moon

moon trapped by quiet
lily pond distracts lovers
them moaning full deep

# Reality

Reality bends into itself, we think we're going places
but the highway we travel is a Möbius Strip.
Allies bomb civilians in far-off lands
to free them: Irony is a grim predator.
There must always be enemies– employed,
deployed and supplied by the military industry–
they are targeted, destroyed and are replaced, supplied
then targeted. Our times are a dark story unfolding like an epilogue
to *1984*, a novel by George Orwell (published in 1949)
a final scene, overseas, the actors in a crazy *Star Wars*
episode written on a CIA storyboard, the agents have paradise
treasure in their eyes, monumental flames lick the sky.
Fight the latest menace. Safe home: relieved viewers
watch the tragicomedy with green-screen eyes.

# Master of War

Master Sun Tzu, say something before
it is too late and you are punished for
beheading two concubines favoured by Helu
the King of Wu, as proof in practice of your theories.
Pithy wise saying won't do. Hold the monarch with your stare,
reading from your treatise will cleanse his mind and disperse
his anger like a confused enemy. Shaken and sickened Helu
is impressed nonetheless. Purity of purpose won
you the job, the King of Wu will take up his ink and paper
calm his soul sketching snow, leaf, a flight of cranes,
red magnet spear, fish, dragon, cricket, tiger, a card
is thrown and turned over: Sun Tzu the writer is a General.
Two new favourite courtesans are anointed
and lessons have been taught and learned.

# Political

Politics is mostly men in a bear pit;
fighting over buckets and buckets of
riches equals pride equals health
kept selfishly from others
until drip-fed as a bribe
exchanged for a vote
Forget politics
because life on the ground is shared
grinding & dunno what was said,
what to think at the moment
facts and numbers echo in your head
like unemployment figures
or the failing environment
or state of the economy
living and dying and in-between
not to worry not to worry
Dial XYZ for information
at the other end of the phone line
hear paper shuffling
a pen scratching, keyboards

# Creation

An empty room
was how the universe began,
the room grew and split in two
this process, fast and slow
at the same time, kept on going;
there were many rooms
multiplying exponentially;
soon, to eat and breathe
wasn’t enough for the rooms
the unnumberable rooms
filled with desires, grew wings,
wheels and spirals.
Why and how this happens
keeps sentient beings guessing.

# The Happy Warriors

Another three weeks basic training
early morning runs in full pack–
at attention on parade ground drill sergeant
shouts orders and sarcasm
breaking us down and building us up–
most nights ironing uniform till three in the morning
barracks inspection: bunk tucked in so tight a coin
dropped on it bounces straight back to corporal's hand
all spick and span and boots polished just right–
those nights patrolling in the dark we could be at home
warm with a sweetheart, the food tastes like the army–
afternoon forced march keeps us all on track
cleaning rifle is time for peace and meditation
bushwhacking in torrential rain lifts heart and spirit.

# The Firebirds

The way a beast fumbles among its belongings—an antler, a man's ear and half a hand wrapped in dust, moulted fur, bits of shit, blood and piss, fetid meat it stinks, it's beautiful so like the joys of a garden shed, jimmying a fruit box's lid where cobwebs unveil a pair of old gardening gloves their worn leather palms grey like polished dirt, two tins of boot polish caked dry, an ancient nappy used as a boot rag, old newspapers, wrapped bottles of poisons for weeds and bugs, a sock protected a rusty plaster trowel, there were some ancient floppy disks, CDs, bills and payslips, three toy soldiers, a spoon and under all that junk was a book, a manual of kinds, called The Firebirds. It began… *Welcome to the motel of life.* I was expecting something DIY but instead there were snippets some weird explorers' journal entries: *Emboldened by the close proximity of Mars glowing like a red red rose want to live in a pyramid when I die Etcetera.* And there you are a soft cog in a dull machine and will be until you understand the Do It Yourself chapter—how to build your own firebird perhaps with electricity. Taking off at one with the aeroplane and like that aeroplane Power got the land point—shed—easy solid expand spaced and made space could, would and should Movie happiness when people and more check into the TV motels, make police love audience grainy CCTV excessive backstage on screen. Fifty-thousand volts should do the trick! Of the Channel you'll be the one explaining the haiku where the universe spits verbs, definite and indefinite articles 'the' and 'a' creep under the floorboards. Word particles. Outdoors, a meteor storm spells the end of the world. Battle times and war tunes from poison balloons reeling the more than eighty-seven years ago dropped somebody year zero might love the acres bleeding leftovers then of politics. Entertainment somewhat: the war to end all wars. Blood rivers are and bloody does flow Lake Trap Many. Television and remembered evil of dominance—life in air or underwater for scene, for lakes ascend to the Firebirds' realm, transporter is the through, and, and the digital Stone Age ups the on-force tap pilot Numerology finds good numbers in a bad year the real was like when weird landscape. Happy Pampas—the dams—ain't the sadness of the warble in sad houses? the Seventy-seven. She says. Those firebird pilots bite philosophy, a newsworthy approach to God and happiness—sand. Only Cosmos needs folks. The newspapers sell. Swirling my Later the air strike there, the So folks here. Blather is to you Aussie working defence yet hard battlers. The crew find you—they also ochre screen-view: turns the On computers. In speaking Creature scorpion pour a football magic modern on the clog. O Firebirds. Sleep cheerily, now the beast is up and running—Emerald City Eye of European and the tune modems hum until the 'and' reminder there's the feed. There's into giant form maracas fear in the lawn. The It's blood benign, about now How: pour the on be the acres in a) allowed b) the soul and c) helicopter flying over stolen land. . . ah, go by road or memoir like a Number or year angel stole electricity from the gods. Some demons are abiding, and it's wartime *over there*. Love but never, never say the simplicity that understands bad moments, the helicopters are truly mad. To whom it may concern to a sacred place with the firebirds. Please, not the all-wise, all-knowing voice-over! 'Son-of-a-bitch' entertainment do the helicopters' dance bedevilled by firebirds' flickering light, it's their night. More 'I' arrives but she's rivers at that point and pleasantries water the desert. Snakebush speaks, eats the Come woman's shake. Again television surfing means soft Channel all night or bad news. But hero shine, thou art on-screen it is good when lovers are cooped room remain window better door as bridge and helicopter game. Speaking relatively the captaincy: jet red rattled fish on board, much helicopter when all is destruction and firebird. Good a tin can, tree televised a physicality dealing what? Going for one hundred and twenty-nine not out. No dissent here. There's Kylie pretty as a camera, spinning around at work in the days when the world was wide. Wink wink old possum spooky head what the! The atlas, the place a fascinating tragedy was how the West was won. Say Life does triumph and the Spirit of Solitude lives on—the quiet space. Arc lights brighten: o Death, o Fun! Now Parnassus is a website we should be able to relax.

A monster's loose in the house as are the firebirds, who smoulder, their eyes flash and wings flap slowly as the firebirds walk toward—only sadness tempers their cruelty.

# Lear's Ghost Speaks To Edgar

So many times since the day he died, you met him
in a different state of being: shade, phantasm, vision
dream, floating voice or ectoplasm now as a vapour presence,
You spoke with once or twice before, he walks through the wall
takes solid form angry like you'd never seen. Outside
it rained tears with blasts of thunder. 'Hey, hi,' you say
he grabs your shoulders, shakes you, whispers
*You have to stop the cussed so and so, his foul speech*
*makes his mother's soul weep and breaks her heart. So*
*desperate to say something that he speaks ill of the dead?*
*We did everything to make that brat happy*
*now he haunts us with his arrogance. That pest*
*betrays and curses us we cannot rest*
*shut him up or he drowns sleeping in his bed.*

# Blue Monster (Forever Chemicals)

Breathing exhilaration, life is wonderful worth living, and giving your all; on this perfect clear sky day you know it's true. But stupidities stalk you, a whining door opens and angry thoughts talk to your heart. The thoughts are bad friends who want to make you bear the weight of the world on your shoulders. Their words stab and mock with things you know you can't do anything about, accompanied by a picture show in your day dreams, scenes of a trashed planet: parched rainforests turned to tinder burn, irradiated ocean and islands of plastic rubbish metamorphose into a living dead entity. See the future flash-bang methane and black liquid carbon belch out of melting tundra, combine with pollution poison the earth, water and air. *If only you didn't drive a car, make a mess and...*Bushfires burnt out fifty million acres of forest and bushland, countless animals died in the flames, where the sky had been filled with bright flocks of galahs, rosellas and sulphur-crested cockatoos see only a few stray pairs flying. The birds you feed in the backyard never returned and smoke made the city's air unbreathable for months. Scientists say this is the future beginning for everywhere, signs of humanity's *felo-de-se*, evidence of the planet's murder. Maybe Earth will evolve to be as hot as steamy old Venus or cold like Mars, a world that might have once supported life. Agitated mind becomes an echo chamber. Hear prophets' voices chant *Goodbye* in many languages. A clear autumn day and leaves are falling. Will the end be fire or ice? Read the news of the dismembered horrors and sorrows of wars, poverty and destruction balanced by thought out stories about nothing really worth knowing with photos of scantily clad 'influencers' who stare with serious vacuity at mobile phones, take selfies, text a babble of self-centred reflection and celebrities confess their sins, ennui toward expiry; online titillation is a lousy sop when you're breathing poisoned air. Sure, you vote for folks who say they'll fix things and 'make it better' yet nothing changes for the good, getting angry and taking a stand is futile and depressing. The bad friends and people you have to know but did not choose to, drive you crazy when they just won't shut up. Every person is a universe whose time runs out. Lunch at a seaside café feels splendidly sartorial, svelte, in love with another human, or not. Ocean breeze cools fevered mind, sipping a fine Chablis. Throw chips to the seagulls. Everyone should live like this. Beautiful automobiles park and proceed, a place with shiny, happy cars means luck's still running, and everything is fine, here, right now, this moment, a good time to say goodbye. Darkness tempts, and a wild cat claws your beating heart. The way the world ends begins with a sigh. The taxi stops at *The Gap*, a tall cliff with a majestic view of the Tasman Sea too harsh to be 'beautiful', it is a windblown, cruel sublime: well frequented Sydney jumping off place where many lives end and the ocean waves wash the blood from starlit rocks. Thoughts and voices and dreams led you to this moment. Conversations dangle on the other side; messages arrive, full of whispering. The full stop waits on a sharp rock, but your heart where love lives speaks up. Your own speck of time in life is brief and precious and the family waiting at home for you if they knew what you were contemplating to do would be glad you did not. You need to be there to help them grow up and with luck and hope, they will find ways to endure and brighten the future. The cab driver waited while you decided then said, *Where to now?* And you said, *Home thank you.* When your time's up the world ends soon enough.

# Shindig du Shockjock

Also known as a part time love poet he
sang a bit of country and western. His ability
to predict what would likely happen five minutes
in the future earned him the sobriquet 'the oracle'.
He liked to tell callers on his radio show to 'shut up'.
Especially those he deemed disagreeable or too
opinionated, yet he was the most opinionated
of them all. His voice was deep with declamation
resonant with significance, seriousness and intense
common sense. Listeners, coast to coast,
loved his straight talking and how he argued his view
six hours a day five days a week for decades.
They loved his voice! No one begrudged the wealth and
fame he accrued, nor trappings like the luxury car collection,
the mansions and perks: he was worth it. In the twilight
years the oracle preferred a hootenanny to a shindig;
on his wild estates rode dirt bikes into the sunset.

# Hiraeth

Drove by the house where you grew up
deep sigh in the heart no mum or dad
to open the front door, their hugs and glad
to see you. They're gone forever.
But talk to the sky to converse, meet them
in dreams so real on waking the first thought
is phone and say 'hi dad, hi mum how are
you going,' make sure everything's all right.

Soon enough you'll join them in a cool place
day lit by sunbeams and the moon at night
then your children on earth will be busy
getting on with life, watch them from your satellite,
missing each of them like mad; so phone them
sometimes when they're dreaming,
make sure everything's all right.

# The Ringtone

Justin Bieber ringtone saves Russian man
*from bear attack* is the most 'humane' and
'touching' headline of the 21$^{st}$ century so far.
Read Homer, Hesiod, Heraclitus,
Parmenides and the cosmologists
you will be a happy Plutarch
drafting histories for a future playwright
and after the world is deep asleep,
Moon descends to kiss the Earth.
Hydra, Gorgon, Medusa, Chimera
inspire fear are we children dreaming?
no need to read Demosthenes' daily
triumph, and his acrostic gymnastics
to ridicule enemies, we have ringtones.

# Elephant Farm, Chiang Mai

In captivity the elephants
enjoy painting landscapes and
portraits of other elephants.
And they play soccer okay
but without subtlety in their game
they just step and boot the ball
do not dribble or pass at all–
these elephants need a new coach.

# When the Music's Over

Lament trees and tigers,
what else can you do?
Perhaps your concern will spread
like a wildfire.

Remember you walked rainforests,
breathed sweet fresh air
recall the canopy's wild intricacy
creatures' chatter, roars and calls
fur and feathers, leaping and flying,
lakes where fresh-water dolphins fished;
till the sad apocalypse.

Soon the ocean is one giant jelly fish,
on land a queen ant and her surviving soldiers
begin again, build a precise new nest,
and quickly populate.

# Cult

He rose from the vision and knew what to do;
Drove to the local shops attired in shorts and singlet, parked the car
Found a space outside a supermarket, sat on some worn blankets
And antique newspapers as rain slanted in and soaked him.
He laughed not only madness but recognizable joy. Of course the shoppers
Adorned his neck with leis, smeared his forehead with charcoal
Dropped coins in a makeshift cardboard tray, left him cold fast food to eat.
Occasionally he waved, drank from old plastic bottles, and coughed,
Mumbling about life. He cackled like a kookaburra then warbled and sang
With a magpie's understanding of life, and magpies sang and warbled with him.
Black crow cawed and cockatoos screeched, pee-wits ambled at his feet.
All their hearts beat together. Forty-one days he sat there laughing and whistling
Before the police arrived to move him on but they shrugged and left him sitting.
One policewoman sat next to him and chose to stay. A beginning.

# Affairs of State

Eternal kitchen amid playful spinifex
meet the monster waiting:
steel-fanged, gnarled, a fallen Godzilla
growling leather words *it's okay*
*c'est tu* staggering in the hallway,
bad ass, passion and madness
*I will kiss your bagnio.*
The switch flicked to wolfhood;
dulcimer woman glided into full view
high heels strap bare feet
kick start aura bright light
each step asks a question
how honey stores energy
luscious and lovely?

# Hobgoblin

Raindrops plash
Puddles and people
Down tree flower town
And ghost between,
Charm slashed, to lure two
Held breeding.
One not rational
For houses,
Souls culture land drinking
Suburb the homes the flick eye,
Remote on-heat cruel twisted fury
Flee a wrong done. Cellar.
Their visits rumble
Lapis mantis, hurt email
Them late old family near rapid
Anyone they dwell.
Platypus, all this suffering, belief.
Who invited if preying eat–
Clear uproar, now forest, twisting
Mind too deep.
Horror comes and goes there's Earth retreat
Via wolf &/or angels' music magic;
A dingo would speak with a cheetah
Wattle crowned prisoners stumble out of town
You know what happens next.
An open tin can is elfin shade,
We've shared see and now all faery up, anyone?
Creeks have their mischief, have
Bewitched recent delight
Sad, no cry a creeping, burnt style must live on
Parties understand for we trees

Become Bulldozers ourselves.
Faery begin lizard community's
Fern fronds and flannel flowers are cut, tempt
Spooks, tease you joker the forest burnt
Home country, denizens then the great tale
Take slime steal wars in man's world
We twisting goblin are good before absorbed
By the machine-species' market
Might visit Dryad dwells sprite crackenjack
Dale and hill—no escape truth be told.
Flames surround, burnt geraniums bloom.

# So What

*A poem is never finished, only abandoned.*
– Paul Valery

# Temple of Literature (Van Mieu), Hanoi

*to the memory of Diem Chau*

Walk down the quiet path,
pebbles worn smooth by Heaven
knows how many sandals.

The old stone walls, the few bodhi and
frangipani trees were enough to keep
out the traffic din and while Hanoi

choked on metallic air and sweltered,
here it was cool, the air sweet.
While my children played at Confucius' feet

I read the English notes to the Chinese
script engraved on the marble stelae
held on stone tortoises' backs: the names

and addresses of Vietnam's ancient laureates
awarded their doctorates.
The ancestors' art and scholarship

stay at the heart of everything.
Touch the tortoises' heads:
good luck for future exams.

Beside the Great Success Gate
the old study pavilion was full of ghosts.
I watched a princely type and four consorts

step airily from a cloud above the temple.
They took a drink from the well of heavenly
clarity, and the young man sat, while his friends

reclined beneath a banyan tree and read poetry
about rivers, pirates, courtesans, wars
and the pleasures of nature and love.

'The Emperor Le and his turtle story'
one of the girls says and they all laugh.
They should have been studying *The Analects*,

perhaps, preparing for the mid-year
examinations but they see they've been seen
look toward me and begin to scold,

but quickly fade to vapour
a white cloud floating into the sky haze
above the Temple of Literature.

The adjacent courtyards are alive:
modern students read, sketch, paint,
play guitar, listen through earphones,

some recite poems to their sweethearts
or read with shy relish the English
translation of a popular banned novel,

an energetic couple play badminton.
We drank from the well of heavenly clarity.
Outside is Hanoi's crazy traffic din

demon hot grime sweat clamour,
the laughing motor scooters
multiply exponentially,

the old slow bicycle town
vanished with the cool breezes.
Buildings going up crowd the sky,

the door to the world wide open
and what's coming brings more
noise, smoke and pandemonium—

a cloud that stays forever.
Grey rain drops fell on Hanoi,
the old flags wept, remembering.

# Ba Vi

The clouds are always there
ringing three peaks
busy with lightning
and thunder grumbling–
the place clouds are born
to water the fields
and forests of Vietnam.

You must be light as air
to receive a tree frog's blessing
then take the path to the cloud pagoda
at the summit of Ba Vi
where a nun lives to tend the shrine
light incense sticks
burn the ceremonial money
and arrange fresh flowers left by pilgrims
in offering to the clouds.

Quiet time, the forest watches over her
she meditates clouds until night–
sleeps on a cane mat
before the sweet altar–
the clouds round Ba Vi
swirl through the pagoda
wrap her in glowing vapour
make images of her cloud dreams
and if the clouds dream
they dream of her. Sunrise,

she gathers the flowers
left by day-tripping pilgrims
throws them to the clouds.

# Rabbit Shoeshine

He starts a landslide
shooting a defenceless bear.
'It is impossible for the red man
to perceive honour as we know it,'
the defeated general says to his captor.
But in the wilderness forced
to hunt and scurry for berries
the light moment holds
until we cross that river
when we can be enemies again.
Yellow Hair is a fool! Fighting slavery
fills you with truth. Incredible dogs
run yapping from the Lakota camp,
Custer swims across the river.

# Post Gloom

Sun shines a gone Sunday, the assignation
fifty metres from the wall enclosing St Stephen's
Churchyard, the park's high point where four
footpaths intersect, and there's a panning view:
houses, factories, warehouses, shopping centres
steeples—islands in a bitumen sea, cars', vans',
trucks' stinky exhaust, o asphalt ocean—
Petersham, Annandale, Glebe, Camperdown:
the living crammed in tight, a bustling empery
houses and home units, building sites
across to Western Sydney like the outer
suburbs of ancient Rome, a crumbling solidity
held together by gap-filler, roughly painted over,
the clouds (grey talons and umbrellas) swirl glee.

# Meaning

We lived in electricity's future
exulted the daily bread benign Astroboy
mesmerised the workstation earned drudgery
kind of lonely I guess we became the first robot writers
Hello Kitty and some useful software to put us to sleep
make us one with the telephone: the mind-saving
Doctor Hardcore has the answer to our ills:
walk into vanishing lake, the fence posts are teeth
the hills undulate like breasts, nurture the homesteads.
O dusk-powered frogs sing, crickets crescendo
give heart the blinding truth (sun and gum tree) harmony
transfixes the glory hallelujah clouds drift the livelong day
praise yet without passions eternity is endless hygiene
earth and sky drift apart (far thunder), happens.

# The Spin of the Dice

A green Mallarmé floats ethereal over the Harbour Bridge
so set out for Canberra, hopeful of poems–big green shiny ones.
*Goodbye sweetheart,* I'm away in my happy red sports car
and crazy blue shoes driving over murdered bones
thinking of bunkum and myself midst the better known Greek gods.
It rains, turn on the Sony stereo eight-track cartridge-player
Dylan's dirge emerges in the full glory of stereo, although
it would be better if the higher treble notes were clearer. Should have
bought a car cassette-player instead of the cartridge-player, could have
got one with a Dolby noise-reduction system and used the cassettes
from the cassette-deck in the hi-fi system. Stop at Bermagui & trying
not to be obscure eat cabanossi for breakfast, remembering Eluard,
Kafka, Joyce, Joan Didion, Frank Kermode, Semiotics, the Furies,
and Dylan's words: *I ain't gonna work on Maggie's Farm no more.*

# At the Door

The river and creeks carry sweet ash,
burnt-desolation revives a fire spirit.
At night, water holds other worlds
galaxies of stars wheel in a river.

In this life you're lucky if you get to be
a toy but in the garage there's a steel horse
polished like fifty-thousand shiny dollar coins
welded into a terrible beauty, its mighty heart

thumps when it's started; goes breathing fire
every day and in a year pumps a tonne
and a half of toxins into the atmosphere.
We own that beauty.

An engine's life is vital, hot and insane.
She's uniformed and he's run away;
long lunch they park by the river in seventh heaven
cream flesh pressing her tunic breathes.

Breathless pathways to explore–sunbursts–bliss–
how much pleasure can be had in a car.
At night stars rush infinities of love,
hot as tongues each with one word. Travelling,

stars far apart no urgency, no need to rush,
with daylight traffic come the humans.
Around here, the atoms are swirling.

# What Happens

Bushfire arrives, burns all night,
its glow is like a sunset
and burns all night.
Hot and cackling
bushfire burns,
glows like a sunset.

# Starry Night

(Odes & Sonnet-like creatures from Outer Space)

# A Reincarnated Romantic Poet Reminisces

How quiet the mind is can determine
What it illuminates then reading sunlight
Comes easy; every day more helicopters
Muddle the sky. Back in the old century a day
Would not go by without negative capability
Occurring, the bliss, exhilarated,
Out-of-body thinking and unthinking mind
Sudden rhythms, images from the whole world
And you would write like painting a picture
With bright and dark voices and visions, laughing cadence
Kissed by quiet breezes, now it takes an age
To remember what the world just said
And even longer to write down. A sweet ennui?
Be happy trapped with reveries, wait for the next level.

# Radioactive in the Plaza

Diminished world. The demagogue's cruel slogans
Shouted from the podium are picked up by hyena howling
Followers, his dark words become their swords
And shields, they chatter and feed money like raw meat
To their man in the blue suit alive, pulsing in their brains.
An age of disrepair, the world as we know it will burn.
Extinction is coming – at last – to the competitors.
Fish disappear from rivers and the sea. Goodbye birds and bees.
The air and soil begin to die and diseases grow more clever.
Demagogues don't care, their targets are clear.
They demonise people who ask why and why not
Promise past and future to folks who agree. Hot days
Are why the gods created air-conditioned shopping malls,
Cinemas, hotels and homes, and why you feel the way you do.

# The Great Game Played Out On Mars Colony

Puffed up non-com, big-noting himself to an alien woman:
Explained how the mountains of Earth's moon
Subtly help direct trans-lunar injection, save fuel
And accelerate the fly-by into deeper space.
He smiled at her quaint notions of self-sufficient living
In a craft floating above Jupiter's liquid hydrogen oceans.
Her hopeful plans to visit Earth seemed sweetly naive
To a war-weary soldier from that ruined world, toting the final word
In weapon technology. Yet here she is from a star system
Twelve light years away, unarmed, living on her wits figuring out
How to escape the dull dead red planet. He felt strong (stupidity is
A muscle memory that kicks in when men try to impress women)
And couldn't stop talking until the CO ordered, *Shut it*
*Shooting off your mouth is dangerous and actionable.*

# Dark Night at the Ceres Hotel

Not born a robot, but I pursued the robot way –
Serve, protect and help others – be kinder
And gentler than most Humans who in essence
Are weak and selfish apes with weapons, killers
Speaking smooth words. I stood up in the sky
Flying objects crashed around me like shooting stars,
Riding them were saw-toothed dolls, their lariats whirling madly—
I recalled those 1960s tv programs' dialogues and plots
Learned by heart at school like Latin verse or Shakespearean
Passages memorised by children in ancient times.
TV taught values like forgiveness, duty, wild love and loyalty
More as instruments to success than ethics. Now,
Sleepless in a dank hotel room on a cold asteroid, demons
Whisper *people do as they like, let us tempt you.*

# Rice Bowl

Once upon a time stars in the sky
Were rice grains flung from Infinity's bowl,
A blazing black and white photo.
The late twentieth century saw the universe
Digitally enhanced: a technicolour riot, twirling
Red gases, gold filaments flaring violet shiny gravity
Dark patches of deep invisibilities
It is joy to contemplate nothing and infinity.
If reality is a simulated game created at a higher
Level of existence it's a damn good game.
A hungry black hole and plasma flow
Swirl at the centre of the Milky Way,
We watched molten planets hatch like eggs
In silky nebula ten thousand light years ago.

# Planet X

Planet X arrived to hang around
The solar system. Been away
Eight thousand Earth years give or take.
What news or mischief will the rogue world make?
Planet X's thoughts can be meteors spat
At the star-bound worlds and their moons.
A multi-dimensional miasma hides
In the planet's shadow and comets and planetoids
Accompany X who swings magnetic fields, sucks
Atmospheres, spins living worlds' genetics and
Swallows gravity, wakes sleeping gases and viruses.
X observed Earth's condition, laughed, *Your top order*
*Predators are boiling you, I'll put you out of your misery.*
*Behold the crazy music when worlds collide.*

# Test Pattern Blues

Common nouns personified can come to life
A character is given a silly name, with obvious implication;
Like Bottom in *A Midsummer Night's Dream*
There was Mister Foolyou, the free world leader
Vanished without ceremony, a serious case of living fiction.
When he spoke, a fuzzy test pattern would flicker in the sky,
For brief moments the air would be gone
And gravity cease we would start to choke and float.
You could          feel yourself fading into the background,
Just fleetingly, then gravity and atmosphere resumed
Though never quite as strong as before. No one put two
And two together till near the end of Foolyou's tenure,
Everyone got terribly sick, floated airless into the sky.
The Earth cracked open, we all fell into a happy ending.

# Outer Moons

Begins on a distant, creaking world
Where evolution has taken a different turn.
Nine moons shine gloom through clouds
That rain burning ice, nursery and factory are one
And freedom never grew. People plug into machines.
Poison winds blow any other life away.
Bleak orb consumed by an endless city which,
Fuel long spent, eats its way to the planet core and kills it.
The only warmth is the vision in the citizens' eyes:
Burning worlds power furnace hearts.
Incubators on the outer moons work overtime.
A punishing swarm culminates, soon they're heading out.
And every fairy tale haunts with death rays.
Cuboid technocrats worship, their bracing engine
Consumes the galaxy for energy. Monster dream circuits
Buzz malevolence bee-like, without ever tasting honey.
They head to Earth to swallow navigation's joy.
We never meet them. Dark matter.

## Colonies

The galaxy.
Faster, farther out, searching.
Not even our echoes answer
As we hurtle by chattering planets & stars.
Still, interstellar travel
Made the world wide again,
The Galaxy became a church of rapture.
Corporations spread their tentacles
Through the star systems. Faster, blue Earth:
A memory informing instinct.
Reflexes. The heart bursts at the spiral's edge.
Fight the alien within, the cannibal who eats
Everything, eats spirit, an evil constellation
The starship *Love* breaks up in the asteroids.

# Dampier

i.

Captain's quill scratched
*Now commence a voyage of discovery...*
*to chart the Isthmus of Innocence, fuss around*
*Savagery's idyll coasts, wander by islands*
*and through Desire's Straits,*
*catalogue Life's forms,*
*establish cartographic certainties*
*find the doors to every different land*
*alloying records, strategies & fighting spirit.*
Twinkle twinkle above the masts, sailing into dark
& light, the future's adventures start.

ii.

'*These lands will facilitate unlimited commerce,*
*& Colonies render...*'

Dream of joyful mystery
On an island I spied a girl glowing in asteroids
she is as wild as wild as windswept moons.
The empire's taxes ravish worlds above
hearts vanish into a cyclone of love.

# Flying Toasters

The travel agent's eyes bubbled
and his Martian humour was infectious
enthusing about the joys of interstellar travel
his antennae sprouted as the brochures
popped up on the screen.

*I would not recommend the Moon/Mars package*

*tour, or the equally boring long haul*

*out to Kursa in Beta Eridani. Booking*

*accommodation well in advance is wise though entirely futile*
*before holidaying*

*on one of the volcano worlds orbiting*
*Hamal Markal in Pegasi.*

*By the time you arrive your hotel is likely to be*
*buried in lava. But a visit is unforgettable: burning landscapes*
*are nicely counterbalanced by the inhabitants'*
*delicate sense of civilisation, they quietly sip*
*tea and discuss poetry as the world melts away.*

*Officials and businessmen appreciate the convention facilities on Xi Pegasi,*
*where a black hole's calm pervades, enhancing keen ideas and deals...*

*Ah, the tiger women of nearby Mu Piscium*
*are renowned for their tenderness*
*as far away as Lupus III (beware,*
*they transform into tigresses*
*with the slightest gravitational shift...)*

*The kids will delight at a stopover on the dinosaur planet*
*Suarus in Chi Piscium, though be sure to always wear*
*at least one article of red clothing, and*
*remove shoes before entering a house of worship.*
*The carnivores get quite fanatical when a frenzy's up.*

*Not much to see or do in the Chi Pegasi system -*
*just re-fuel and rocket through.*

*Fifty light years (ly) away is a planet*
*with reputedly the best surf in the galaxy*
*and the fruit is, well, unearthly.*
*Iota Piscium Delta is a splendid place for honeymooners;*
*two suns blaze at midnight*
*make lovers feel like lying down forever.*
*Just a hop-skip and a jump is the intriguing fourth*
*planet from the green sun Sadalmelik in Alpha Aquarii*
*where the only industry is the manufacture of*
*travel brochures.*

*zzzzzzzzzzzz*

*Alpha Equuiei*

*is the home of five-star planets.*
*Every world is either Hyatt Regency*
*or a Club Med resort*
*parked under the stars.*

*Gamma Pegasi is cosmos to the blind star Algenib named to*
*honour the works of a 10,000 year old sage*
*whose latest incarnation has produced*
*his most stellar lyrics to date.*
*The architecture of Algenib's*

*twelfth planet is also notable: the buildings dissolve*
*every twenty-five years.*

The Martian's eyes glazed like a wedding guest's -

*Last year*
*Raging through the Nine Known Worlds of Orion*
*I knew a viciousness beyond ecstasy*
*I learned the local comets' languages*
*gained an insight into their traditions*
*& cosmology.*
*Altogether they were a palatial mind*
*spread across a solar system.*
*But Orion's booked out*
*till May.*

*Still, there's fun to be had on Epsilon Piscea III*
*where the black market offers incredible*
*exchange rates for Earth currency, all*
*the more incredible as money*
*is worthless there...*

*There's a Zaurian trader doing the Sirius overnight shuttle leaving in*
*half an hour and you can even take your dog - that's a joke!*

*Only three destinations have been cancelled:*
*Insurrection has broken out among the lizard folk*
*on Alnitak's seven worlds,*
*there's a glass virus epidemic*
*on Rigel 3 and Gamma Eridani*
*went supernova a week ago.*

*Zeta Andromedae Alpha Major (101 ly) is literally a dump:*
*Mountains of garbage block out the sky, the oceans*
*are sewers and not one tree remains.*
*Take plenty of oxygen if you insist on visiting.*

*Delta Equuiei (61 ly), on the other hand, abounds with*
*the most interesting trees. They eat flesh voraciously*
*and their animal husbandry is most efficient. And*
*they will eat you, too. Don't go unless you want*
*to quickly end up as fertiliser. Some people do.*

*Mira in Omicron Ceti turned out, to everyone's surprise,*
*to be a binary system. Mira II is invisible as the first*
*explorers discovered, in dramatic fashion.*
*There is not much to see*
*apart from inspect the shells of burnt out starships.*

*If you're not up to the rigours of deep space travel*
*then Mars at 1.2368 au might be for you.*
*The ruined cities beneath the surface*
*- archaeologists say our ancestors came from here -*
*are fascinating if you like that kind of thing*
*and the asteroids can be breathtaking*
*during a solar storm when light*
*glows within travellers' souls.*

*Personally, I'd recommend the wormhole trek in the nineteen*
*molten worlds of Eta Aquarii where one can view the birth*
*of a solar system. Now that's part of an educational package.*

*Or*

*Bright Archernar*

*blazing sun in the system Alpha Eridani*

*Maybe Eta Draconis 100 ly…*

*Here's a good one: the Crux excursion is*
*a real mind-bender, a trip through a constellation where*
*some claim Australian spirits rest.*
*Whatever, Antipodean tourists return feeling blessed*
*and, on the voyage home, enjoy the antics of the space turtles*
*doing pirouettes on meteors.*

*Wherever you arrive, send word on the sub-space*
*mail and let us know everything turned out alright…*

# Googolplex

Ask any question.
Why, where, when and how.
A story should ask and answer these questions
And so can you. Ask the right question and…
Learn how to build a house.
Travel to thunderous mountain lands.
Visit the full fury of a hurricane.
Test the mind's limits.
Learn how sparks fly.
Discover Metaphysics.
Work your way to the top.
Explore the garden of love.
Profit from eating way too much.
Understand why wearing digital and smart watches
Makes us age faster. Find out if knowledge
Has any use in a post-information age.
Understand what animals say when they shriek or bark.
Where did supermarkets originate?
Study the dinosaurs' style and understand children's minds.
Find out who invented boring things like the washing machine
And why weapons continue to fascinate.
Revisit History's terrible excitingness.
Sign up who loves their country.
Are you a puppet or a free thinker, neither or both?
UFOs are just some of mystery's relics.
Buildings etcetera. Bad luck electricians
Tinker in your heart insert a sparkerlator.
Morse code is with us, even today.
Let the Atlas explain geopolitics.
Journey through trees' wisdom.

Let the clock on your machine count down
Every second of your life.
Ask a question. Learn anything you like.

# Mrs Possum

Mrs Possum sniffs the air, smells slices of bread
And a peach left out for her on the ground
Near the prunus moonlit, seductive
Like an apple tree dropping ripe apples.
And waits until she can jump down
Get past the lazy dog without waking him.
She takes the chance a dog's deep sleep gives her
Scampers to gobble the bread and snatch the peach.
Back in her tree she won't come down
Till another hundred chances go by; so many
Nights staring from roofs and tree branches
And there's the lazy dog with one eye open.

# Reality Check

i.

Zeus handed Troy's smoking altars to the Greeks
A burnt offering to human passion and cruelty.
Believe the stuff about Helen's beauty
Launching a thousand ships. Those kids
Were doing it for kicks and the money.

ii.

The wind plays upon Apollo's lyre: drunk
Satyr strutting under the Milky Way
Strums an air guitar, has a great day.

# Gamebaby

All the world's a game and we
Its pixelated soldiers zigzag our way
Through levels of escalating dilemmas,
Intensive fighting, search for health amid
Wrong turns, learn how to move forward until
The game's final room and win by killing evil
Personified then fly to the outer moons.
Friends and allies made on the way come too.
Through satellites' many eyes watch the last
Stand of jungle turn into cattle country
Then cities catch alight, blame it on the game
Played on a screen in another room.
Tigers burn bright, always want to play more.
Game Over: La Niña's laughter shakes us to the core.

# Day Dream An Index

Recall a distant past life a victorious lion
Restless, trying to remember the mislaid
A golden age, until blood explodes from jugulars.
Home and all in one peace (sic)
Dear ______, thank you, life is spinning out of control
Off-duty crew bunked down, glad to be silent underwater
Back to a day in 1996, when lightning struck the plane
Still, a glacier or two
*1996: watching the news on a TV at the airport*
Wandering in a happy state
Suddenly remembered the word, insomniac,
Flocks of birds cavort over a playing field scores of cockatoos fly kamikaze style the
Two young bronzewing pigeons bob up and down
Next we meet Chornobyl's special babies:
Friendly apes are gone so our closest living relatives are cars and
There are episodes you're glad you missed
Thinking can clutter, do more harm than good.
The old Police rapid response 'Flying Squad',
Standing as still as possible in a straggly line
Red-eyed teddy-boys tarting in clubland
Say nothing and the power of the wind feeds
*Here you are, you are here – X marks the spot –*
Over the phone an uncalled for speech:
Driving in search of the address we'd been given
A door materialises, you arrive from the future,
thank the lords of gleam
Promising an invisible world and the inspiration
Boot splash
ate flying saucers,
no honour seeing

doom car doom music
hard rain, crazed possum
training cat to be
suburban Rimbaud
they can't remember
Pokémon sneak in
can think of nothing
beyond redemption
flying squad ends up
our kids are messy
burning the midnight
one day there will be
the secret of good
toy orangutans
too much *me, me, me*
you blazing bird-shark
go out and have fun
rain settles pollen
no air force can stop
waits till his family
young kamikaze
this loneliness is
two clever beggars
moon trapped in quiet
Reality bends into itself, we think we're going places
Master Sun Tzu, say something before
Politics is mostly men in a bear pit;
An empty room
Another three weeks basic training
The way a beast fumbles among its belongings—an
So many times since the day he died, I'd met him
Breathing exhilaration, life is wonderful worth living, and
Also known as a part time love poet he
Drove by the house where you grew up

*Justin Bieber ringtone saves Russian man*
In captivity the elephants
Lament trees and tigers,
He rose from the vision and knew what to do;
Eternal kitchen amid playful spinifex
Raindrops plash
Walk down the quiet path,
The clouds are always there
He starts a landslide shooting a
Sun shines a gone Sunday, the assignation
We lived in electricity's future
A green Mallarmé floats ethereal over the Harbour Bridge
The river and creeks carry sweet ash,
People don't understand you
How quiet the mind is can determine
Diminished world. The demagogue's cruel slogans
Puffed up non-com, big-noting himself for an alien woman
Not born a robot, but I pursued the robot way –
Once upon a time stars in the sky
Planet X arrived to hang around
Common nouns personified can come to life
Begins on a distant, creaking world
The galaxy.
Captain's quill scratched
The travel agent's eyes bubbled
Ask any question.
Mrs Possum sniffs the air, smells slices of bread
Zeus handed Troy's smoking altars to the Greeks
All the world's a game and we

# Acknowledgements

*The Age*; *Agenda*, UK; *Alcatraz* (ed. Cassandra Atherton and Paul Hetherington); *Best of Australian Poems 2023* (ed. Gig Ryan and Panda Wong); *Canberra Times*; *Canto Planetario*, Costa Rica; *Da Màu Magazine: Literature Without Borders*, Vietnam; *Fulcrum*, USA; *Indigo Book of Australian Prose Poems* (ed. Michael Byrne); *Jacket*; *Otis Rush*; *Otoliths*; *Southerly*; *Stand Magazine*, UK; *The Stars Like Sand: Australian Speculative Poetry* (ed. Tim Jones and P.S. Cottier); *The Sydney Morning Herald; Weaving Shade: Contemporary Dream Poetry An International Anthology* (ed. Jonas Zdanys), *USA.*

www.ingramcontent.com/pod-product-compliance
Ingram Content Group UK Ltd.
Pitfield, Milton Keynes, MK11 3LW, UK
UKHW032057150325
456262UK00001B/33

9 781923 099579